M000103621

Forever Grateful To You:

Made in the USA
Middletown, DE
22 October 2020

22612750R00066